JESUS,
HIS LAST WILL AND TESTAMENT

pasquale foresi

Pasquale Foresi

JESUS,
HIS LAST WILL
AND TESTAMENT

meditations on unity, faith,
hope and charity

New City London

First published as '*Il testamento di Gesu*' 1966
by Città Nuova, Rome

First published in Great Britain 1986
by Mariapolis Ltd
57 Twyford Avenue, London W3 9PZ
© 1986 New City London

Cover picture, Westphalian Master, ca.1380.
Pentecostal picture. 'Wallraf-Richartz-Museum, Cologne'.

ISBN 0 904287 27 0

Nihil Obstat: R.C. John Redford STL LSS, censor
Imprimatur: + Charles Henderson VG
            Southwark 26th June 1986

Set in Great Britain by Chippendale Type,
   Otley, West Yorkshire
Printed and bound in Great Britain by Biddles Ltd.,
   Guildford and King's Lynn

Contents

Introduction

'The first fruits of all the Scriptures are the Gospels', wrote Origen, 'and the first fruit of the Gospels is the Gospel of St. John'. We could add to Origen's beautiful thought, 'and the first fruit of John's Gospel is the Testament of Jesus, his prayer recorded in chapter 17'.

It confronts us with one of the most intimate moments of his life. On the one hand, he appears in his earthly existence as the revealer of his humanity, in his invitation to conversion, to love, to mercy, to human solidarity: on the other, as in this prayer, he reveals his divinity, his full communion with the Father.

Chapter 17 has been defined as a 'last will and testament'. It is his prayer to the Father before the passion, full of supernatural and divine meaning, a priestly prayer. Jesus does not pray for himself or for the world, but, 'for those whom you have given me', 'that they may be perfectly one', as he is with the Father. He prays for all future believers, so that all may be one.

His prayer becomes universal, embracing the whole of mankind. He declares his unity with the Father and offers himself to men as *the* perfect revelation. He asks his disciples to live in the truth of God, made holy by faith in the Father and by unity. Finally, he prays for the Church of believers reunited by the witness of the Apostles.

How can people of today enter into the heart of the message of Jesus? How can they know the Word, the truth? 'This is eternal life, that they may know you, the only true God and Jesus Christ whom you have sent'. The *lived* understanding of the Word, of the Testamant of Jesus, provides the basis for understanding the Gospel. Understanding Jesus in these words can be a gateway to understanding the whole Gospel.

These meditations of Pasquale Foresi on the Testament of Jesus and on faith, hope and charity in the New Testament, can help us to discover a deep intimacy with God in the *lived* experience of every day. As Scripture presents him, Jesus is a living person. He is *life*. To have a relationship with him, the author invites us to become his Word, the Word who comes to life within us.

The Editor.

The Testament of Jesus

Father the time has come. Glorify your Son, that your Son may glorify you. For you granted him authority over all men that he might give eternal life to all those you have given him. Now this is eternal life, that they may know you, the only true God, and Jesus Christ, whom you have sent. I have brought you glory on earth by completing the work you gave me to do. And now, Father, glorify me in your presence with the glory I had with you before the world began.

I have revealed your name to those whom you gave me out of the world. They were yours, you gave them to me and they have obeyed your word. Now they know that everything you have given me comes from you. For I gave them the words you gave me and they accepted them. They knew with certainty that I came from you, and they believed that you sent me.

I pray for them, I am not praying for the world, but for those you have given me, for they are yours. All I have is yours, and all you have is mine. And glory has come to me through them. I will remain in the world no longer, but they are still in the world, and I am coming to you, Holy Father, protect them by the power of your name – the name you gave me – so that they may be one as we are one. While I was with them, I protected them and kept them safe by that name you gave me. None has been lost except the one doomed to be lost, thus was Scripture proved true.

I am coming to you now, but I say these things while I am still in the world, so that they may have the full measure of my joy within them. I have given them your word and the world has hated them, for they are not of the world any more than I am of the world. My prayer is not that you take them out of the world but that you protect them from the evil one.

They are not of the world, even as I am not of it. Sanctify them in the truth, your word is truth. As you sent me into the world, I have sent them into the world. For them I sanctify myself, that they too may be sanctified in the truth.

My prayer is not for them alone. I pray also for those who will believe in me through their word, that all of them may be one, Father, just as you are in me and I am in you. May they also be one in us so that the world may believe that you have sent me. I have given them the glory that you gave me, that they may be one as we are one;

I in them and you in me, so that they may be brought to perfect unity to let the world know that you sent me and have loved them even as you have loved me.

Father, I want those you have given me to be with me where I am, and to see my glory, the glory you have given me because you loved me before the creation of the world.

Righteous Father, though the world does not know you, I know you, and they know that you have sent me. I have made your name known to them, and will continue to make it known so that the love you have for me may be in them and that I myself may be in them. (Jn. 17, 1-26.)

Knowing God

'And this is eternal life,
that they may know you,
the only true God
and Jesus Christ whom you have sent'.
(Jn. 17,3.)

We need to approach these words reported by St John and spoken by our Lord at the Last Supper in a spirit of humility and adoration, love and fear.

In them Jesus has described eternal life and told us how to reach it. Small wonder that the scholars have subjected each one to loving analysis, the better to sound its depth and grasp its precise meaning.

What does *eternal life* mean or rather what does *life* mean?

St Thomas Aquinas in his commentary on this passage of John analyses the content of the word *to live* and states that since intelligence is *life* and understanding is *living*, it follows that in paradise eternal life is a never ending understanding of God, the very object of that life. Seeing God forever and so rejoicing in this divine understanding – this is the meaning of the word *life*.

Yet we may wonder whether eternal life, this life which is such an immediate experience of God that it permits us to say that we live in him, begins only after death or whether we may hope it to begin here below.

It begins here on earth. This is what the verb 'that they may know' tells us. *That they may know* is a present tense and so has its beginning here on earth. And the present also indicates that this knowledge will not be once and for all but will continue and never be exhausted. The *knowing* of eternal life will always be a novelty: we shall never be able to say 'enough'.

And the word *to know* as used by John, is not mere speculation. It expresses a fullness of life which goes beyond mere understanding. It includes affection of the mind, esteem, respect and therefore charity. In fact, for John love is the root of the knowledge of God. ('Everyone who loves ... knows God. He who does not love has not learnt to know God, because God is love'. (1 Jn. 4,8.))

But in John the word *to know* means even more. It corresponds to 'belonging to the family group and friends of God and of Christ'. It is equivalent to being his sons, as is evident from Jesus' famous description of himself:

'I am the Good Shepherd and *I know my sheep and mine know me*, just as the Father knows me and I know the Father'. (Jn. 10,14–15.)

So knowing implies a living union with God and with Jesus Christ and we can see why *to know* is the definition of eternal life, since it implies an act of intelligence which includes love, giving, belonging and possessing. This passage also tells us that the one we must know like this, possess like this, is 'the only true God'. The words *only true* stress opposition to the multiplicity of false, lying and deceitful gods of the pagans, whilst John insists that the God of the Christians is the God of truth, the God of the Word. So his faithful will be lovers of the true, adorers in spirit and in truth.

'And Jesus Christ whom you have sent'.

Anyone who knows God knows the Word made flesh, Jesus who presents himself to us as the one sent, the Messiah. For Christians, knowledge of God, belonging to him means knowing and recognizing the incarnate Son of God, seeing him, like the Father, as the *only true God*. The conjunction *and* in fact places the one sent by God on the same level as the one who sends him. So to Christians will fall the same loving, adoring knowledge and recognition and acceptance of the mystery of the incarnation.

These words are also words of life given by the Holy Spirit, and not just abstract and speculative truths. Knowledge of them must lead us to live and ponder them attentively. This does not appear difficult, since the eternal life we must know, begins here on earth. As has been said, knowing God is not a question of setting out to study theology and Sacred Scripture, as if it were a science like mathematics or philosophy. This kind of knowing is within everyone's reach.

It means seeing things with the eye of God and so possessing an attentive and watchful spirit of faith. A spirit of faith that will make us look at our problems, great or small, in a different way.

Then all my acquaintances and neighbours, however pleasant or unpleasant, under the divine gaze given by faith, will be so many people in whom to glimpse the face of Jesus. Loving them and helping them, I shall love Christ, I shall love God. *I shall know eternal life.*

With the supernatural eye of faith, I shall not only accept sorrows, difficulties and poverty, but I shall be able to thank the Lord for them, since they will give me a way of resembling more closely him who actually chose poverty and suffering, the better to manifest his divine work on earth.

Everything changes under the new gaze infused into us by the grace of baptism. And yet we are often tempted to look at things in a human way, as though we were not Christians at all.

Then it will be for me to live these words within me, pondering them always in my heart, continually renewing my mentality, my intelligence, with a new outlook.

Little by little, even my soul will form the habit of seeing things with the eye of God and it will become normal for me to look at everything through his eyes. So life will appear more logical and simple, more beautiful and profound.

After an initial effort, if I live in the supernatural for any length of time, it will become natural for me to live in the world of the 'spirit', as St Paul says, and no longer in the world of the 'flesh'.

So putting into practice this word of Jesus can give us the opportunity to accustom ourselves to a new way of living, acquiring that spirit of divine wisdom which will allow us to know and love the only true God and Jesus Christ whom he has sent. That spirit of wisdom and understanding which teaches us to distinguish between the true and the false, the living and the dead, the real and the unreal. A spirit of wisdom and understanding, given us by the Lord to guide us in our family duties and in our duties at work, whether as manager or employee. A spirit of wisdom and understanding that will direct all our actions always and only towards knowing and loving God, that is, to eternal life.

Perfecting His Glory

'I have glorified you on earth
and finished the work
you gave me to do.
Now, Father, it is time for you to glorify me
with that glory I had with you
before the world was'.
(Jn. 17,4–5.)

As always when John reports the words of Jesus, their depth escapes us. Here the Word continues his dialogue with the Father and even if he speaks as man, he uses words of an infinite richness and wisdom.

To try and plumb their depth we must seek the help of the Fathers and scholars down the centuries.

'I have glorified you on earth'.

The glorification of God is a term with various meanings in both the Old and New Testaments. It indicates men's loving knowledge of the Most High, the recognition of his almighty power and majesty. So we might think that the Master's words, 'I have glorified you upon earth', means simply – I have preached your name, I have spoken about you, I have made you known. But further on in his dialogue, Jesus describes exactly how he brings about the glorification of his Father: 'I have finished the work you gave me to do'.

The Greek word John uses would be better translated: 'I have completed the work you gave me to do'. So the Lord glorified the Father on earth not so much by preaching as by exposing himself to his passion and death. As he ends his life, he fulfils and consummates the work which will glorify the Father on earth. We may note with St Augustine that the evangelist does not say – the work you commanded me to do, but the work you gave me to do.

In God everything is love, even his commands, even the tasks he gives to men and above all to the Son of Man. And this gift always implies a voluntary acceptance on the part of the receiver of the command, so that the consequent glory may be true and deep.

Jesus is not yet dead when he utters these words, on the eve of his arrest and crucifixion. For him the consummation has already begun, is already in operation, and he now sees it happening.

The prayer continues: 'Now, Father, it is time

for you to glorify me'. Jesus, speaking with the Father, sees and requests his glorification as man. Just as the glorification of the Father does not consist only in spreading the news about him among men, so the glorification of the Son will not be brought about by human words and rumour, but will be that same glory which the Father had reserved for him as man and predestined for him even before the world began.

This interpretation of St Augustine and St Thomas that the glory our Lord requests, is the very same as that planned for him as man from eternity in the bosom of the Father, completes and blends with the other interpretation of many great scholars and theologians, namely that the glory with which the humanity of Jesus will be resplendent, will be the very same as that enjoyed by the Word from all eternity in the bosom of the Father. It will be a reflection of the divinity that will penetrate more fully the flesh of the Risen Christ, making him the instrument of the omnipotent grace of the Most High.

Both interpretations, in fact, coincide in the request of Jesus to the Father. He asks that once his death has completed the work of the Father's glorification, his own glorification may follow on, giving his humanity that divine power which the Word has enjoyed from eternity in the heart of the Trinity.

However deep these words of the Gospel may be, they are not difficult to live.

Like Jesus, each one of us must glorify the Father and, as with him, the glory we give should not be merely our spoken witness before men. Certainly this helps. Expressing openly with love our own Christian convictions about eternal truths or about particular facts has its place, but the glory each one of us can give to the Father, will consist in completing and consummating what God expects of us.

As soon as the use of reason permits us to learn the truths of faith, our task is to carry out that plan, that command, that personal call of God to us as we entered the world. Each one of us has to complete his mission. Often we ourselves are ignorant of it, as we seem powerless to realize our plans and desires. At times our lives appear as flat and monotonous as everyone else's and we are driven to ask ourselves, 'What can I say to the world to glorify the Father? What can I possibly add to the chorus of mankind?'

And yet it remains profoundly true that in the plan of God each one has to fulfil his mission. Our task may seem great or small, but it is one no one else can accomplish because from all eternity God has loved and predestined us for that very reason.

So it will not be by words but through a life full of Christ, fulfilling all his general and particular wishes for us, that we shall bring to completion the work he has given to us with love and out of love.

Once completed, like Christ we shall be able to ask the Father to grant us that glory reserved for us in the Trinity since before the world began.

From all eternity God has been thinking of us and of our glory, that glory which, our task on earth done, he has in mind for us in paradise after death and after the final resurrection.

The resurrection of Christ and the glory of his body were realized immediately because in him there was the fullness of all mankind, whereas for us the fullness of glory will only follow at the end of time when together with all the elect, we shall make up the Mystical Body of Christ. Then, our flesh too will share in that glory radiating from the divinity of the Word, the Son of God, that glory which has begun here on earth with the fulfilment of each one's mission.

The Mystery of the Name

'I have made your name known to the men
you gave me'.
(Jn. 17,6.)

This word describes the mission of Jesus. He came to make known the name of the one who sent him.

The depth of this statement will be better understood if we remember that throughout antiquity, in particular among the Jewish people, *the name* was not just a sound of the voice used to distinguish one person from another, one thing from another, as is often the case with our modern Western concept.

Among the Semites, *the name* was thought of as the deep expression of the reality of the person who bore it. It was the 'manifestation' of his being before men.

This idea was so deeply rooted that we find it in the first chapters of Genesis, where it is written that: "God from the soil fashioned all the wild beasts and all the birds of heaven. These he brought to the man to see what he would call them; each one was to bear the name the man would give it'. (Gen. 2, 19.)

It is obvious that Adam was not simply invited by God to allot different sounds to each animal. Rather, according to the purpose of each living thing, he had to express its characteristic by means of the name.

It was still a period when the value of language was profoundly linked to the nature of things.

The same will happen to Abram whose name meant 'of noble origin'. It will be changed to Abraham because 'I will make you the father of a multitude of nations'. (Gen. 17,5.)

We find the same motive behind the People of Israel never daring to utter the name of God (Yahweh = 'I am who I am'). To do so would have been a sacrilege, since it would have revealed his majesty and his omnipotence outside the temple.

This idea is present throughout the story of Israel until Christ who also, through the name, wished to indicate the mission, definition and aim for which a person is born and lives.

When Simon was introduced to him, 'Jesus looked hard at him and said: "You are Simon son of John; you are to be called Cephas – meaning Rock"'. (Jn. 1,42.) Precisely because on Peter, the Rock, the Lord was building the Church, the new temple of Jerusalem, visible upon earth.

So when, at the Last Supper, he turned to heaven and said: 'I have made known your name to men', he expressed all the depth and grandeur of his mission as revealer of the name of God.

And what is the name that he has made known, what is the essence, the nature he has revealed to us?

He has revealed that God is Father. So he has fulfilled his mission. He has made known to the world that the Lord who is in heaven, the almighty Creator of all things, is our Father who loves us tenderly, one by one, with an immeasurable and unimaginable fervour towards us.

Jesus has revealed that 'God is the Father of us men', even though we are sinners.

For this very reason he has sent his only Son, so that we may be rescued from sin.

The Church has always maintained the worship and profound veneration for the mystery of the name that we find in the Christian religion.

The feast of the name of Jesus exists to signify precisely this: in divine things the name expresses the reality.

Now, at the end of his life, Jesus can say that he has fulfilled his mission because he has revealed the immense love of God for men. He has made it known that God is love, is Father.

But the passage continues with another expression: 'I have made known your name *to the men you took from the world to give me'*.

At that moment he turns to the Twelve who are listening to him, the Twelve who are to be the founders of the twelve tribes of the new Israel, that is, of all mankind. Through them and their efforts, he will reach the ends of the earth. He describes the Twelve and in them all Christians, as persons whom the Father has taken from the world. This is not to be understood in a negative way. From eternity every Christian has been chosen beforehand by the love of God and consecrated like Paul, even before birth, to be a child of the Father.

If we could manage to grasp only a little of the greatness of the Christian vocation, our lives, mediocre and ordinary as they often are, would change. Before the world began, a pre-existent choice and an infinite plan was present for each one of us, despite our miseries, our weaknesses and our sins.

And like our Lord, we also by our lives and our co-operation must reveal to men his name, his fatherhood, in order to continue with the disciples of the Apostles, our bishops, to bring forth from the world many others and introduce them to the mystery of their being chosen, of their true names.

The Mystery of the Word

'For I have given them the words you gave to me, and they have accepted them and have truly known that I came from you'.
(Jn. 17,8.)

Throughout the Gospel of John the 'Word' has a unique resonance, with a sound different from the one we are accustomed to. From the very first verses of the Gospel, John presents us with God who is the Word. 'In the beginning was the Word and the Word was with God and the Word was God'.

So it comes as no surprise that in the last discourse of Jesus, his 'words' have a profound meaning. They are not simply material sounds conveying an idea, or a concept. Often in our conversation the idea expressed in words does not correspond faithfully to the reality of things, but transforms and alters them the moment it is uttered.

In John the 'words' have their most profound human and divine significance. The 'words' tell us precisely the substance of the things they express. There is neither discrepancy nor alteration; the 'words' expressed do not deceive us. This is because, together with an idea, they contain a nuance and a potential of moral value.

The 'words' of John are not just expressions of the true, but also of the good. Within their articulated sounds this particle of truth and goodness contains a luminous quality which is carried and communicated to the listeners.

Here appears another wonderfully deep power of the 'word' in John's Gospel. It penetrates the souls of those who work for good, that is of those who do the truth, whereas it is rejected by those who love themselves and all injustice.

In the whole of the Fourth Gospel we witness this struggle between the 'word' and the lie: 'If you remain in my word, you will truly be my disciples and you will know the truth and the truth will make you free'. (Jn. 8,31-32.) And Jesus again to the Jews: 'Why do you not understand my language? Why do you not hear my words? You have the devil as your father and you wish to accomplish the desires of your father...in him there is no truth'. (Jn. 8, 43-44.)

But the 'word' does not have only a human content of truth and goodness. There is not only a line of division between the good who receive it and the wicked who try to suffocate it. The 'word' of Christ contains something divine within itself.

It is the Johannine theology of the Word who is God made flesh, flowering again. The human 'words' of the Word are like containers, capable of carrying God himself into souls and making men divine. The eternal Word by means of the human 'words' of Christ makes men eternal: 'In truth I tell you, whoever keeps my word will never see death'. (Jn. 8, 51.)

The person who accepts the 'word' of God, welcomes God into himself. Because of this, Sacred Scripture, the supreme 'word' of God, will be one of the means of spreading truth, goodness and salvation among humanity down the centuries.

This is why when Jesus says to the Father, 'I have given them the words which you gave to me', he is not just revealing thereby that the deposit of ideas and true concepts has been sown in the heart of the Apostolic college, the Church. He is saying that the very life of God is henceforth in the hands of the disciples of Jesus, who will hand it on from generation to generation till the end of time.

He Prayed for His Own

'I pray for them....
for those you have given me'.
(Jn. 17,9.)

The whole sentence uttered by Jesus is more precise. 'I pray for them; I am not praying for the world, but for those you have given me because they belong to you'.

Jesus, at this moment turns to the Father, wishing to pray for his disciples, for those who had welcomed him and accepted his word, becoming his own and his Father's.

That is why he says: 'I do not pray for the world'.

This statement has led some people to interpret the word 'world' in a completely negative and hostile sense. The world is seen as everything that is evil, all that is far from God and under the power of the devil.

But a closer look at this expression reveals no

wish to condemn. Rather has Jesus come to save the world (3,16).

The best scholars maintain that by 'world' Jesus meant human beings as a whole whom he certainly loved and would wish to save; but here he wishes to express special prayer for his friends, for his disciples.

This is a very important shade of meaning. Here we see Christ not as a symbolized abstraction of an individual having to save only universal and cosmic man. Certainly, Jesus is also the redeemer of the universe, but his humanity is complete and rich in all the nuances of feeling and affection of a real man, of any normal man.

Perhaps just because of this, before he dies, he turns to his Father and prays for his own, for those who have followed him in his apostolic journeying along the roads of Judea and Galilee, for those who had shared with him the fatigues and the thirst, the threats and deceit of the Pharisees.

Between Jesus and his disciples there had been established a relationship not just of redeemer with the redeemed, of founder of the Church with her future leaders, but also that of a father with his sons, of a master with his disciples, of a friend with his friends.

It is this perfection of humanity that is heard throbbing in the divine words of the mysterious prayer of Jesus to the Father. It is this wholeness that gives us a deeper insight into the way we should practise our faith.

Above all, if by now we have understood the importance of the apostolate and the value of Christian witness, we can more easily appreciate how our Christian relationships with others can never afford to be either disembodied or cold and unfeeling.

Jesus demands of us a completeness of human feelings inspired by the divine, so that we can appreciate and understand everyone, non-believers included, realizing how Jesus neither destroys nor limits man but raises and completes him.

Therefore, we owe our own people, those closest to us, a special affection, with a special place in our prayers.

And in the Church no one should ever feel himself to be alone.

The Church is not a cold and schematic organisation, but the home of the children of God. It is the family where the bonds of blood have been completed and surpassed by the bonds of the Holy Spirit who has come down on us and made us brothers and sisters.

In the Church, then, when her nature is lived out, we feel at home and we have that intimacy with the Father, with Jesus and Mary which befits children who feel the deep divine and human bonds that enrich them.

How distant is true Christianity from that

cold, negative concept which the puritan and Jansenistic traditions wished to offer us!

What is Mine is Yours

*'All mine is yours
and all yours is mine'.*
(Jn. 17,10.)

'What is mine, is yours'. Jesus as second divine
Person, continues in human words his eternal
dialogue with the Father. For us, a mysterious
dialogue that only Jesus, as the second Person
made flesh, could have revealed. In this dialogue
there is the entire gift of the Father to the Son and
the whole gift of the Son to the Father. It is the
deepest law of the Trinity revealed to us.

In the most Holy Trinity the mutual and
reciprocal gift of the Persons is total and perfect.
Theology tells us that everything is in common,
except that which properly distinguishes fatherhood from sonship. This 'everything' is not
merely one but unique. Unique is the divine
reality which the Father transmits to the Son in
generating him and which the Son receives as the

37

one generated. Unique too is their breath of love that is the Holy Spirit.

These are thoughts and words steeped in mystery. Theology has tried to explain them to us, but naturally without much success. So the words of Christ which open up his relationship with the Father, will always remain a continuous discovery, for ever luminous and obscure at the same time.

But these words and their reality, in so far as we can grasp it, have been revealed for us to live them.

Jesus desired to externalize his divine, eternal dialogue with the Father, for it to be food and motive of our life.

So then, for us Christians as well, this is the deepest and most vital law: 'All that is mine is yours, all that is yours is mine'. They are words of truth for everyone who believes in the message of Christ.

A deep communion of spiritual goods binds us all together. The divine trinitarian life has already been poured into our hearts and has become the law of our life here on earth.

But this norm does not affect our spiritual lives. The communion of saints must not remain just a formula of the Creed. It must be the inspiration of the whole of our daily life, even in material and practical things.

God has given us the goods of the universe for the good of all, so that all may share in this love of God for their human and Christian sustenance. But in order to safeguard the liberty and dignity of individuals, he wishes the goods of this earth to be at the service of all, generally by means of what is called private property.

Nonetheless, private property must not be a means and a location to preserve selfishness and avarice.

Private property is a service that each one should perform for the good of the community.

Yet how far we are from the reality of the true idea of private property, which has its roots in the trinitarian mystery so perfectly expressed in: 'All yours is mine and all mine is yours'. What a deformation of this concept the words and lives of many Christians offer! It is appealed to as a 'sacred' right, not to give more to others but to be more selfish and grasping. Often this property right is claimed in order to remove completely other people's right to 'private property' in the name of one's own liberty, independence and personality.

Are the scourges of revolution really necessary to remind us what true Christianity is? Are we incapable of being renewed simply by living up to the Gospel? Let us hope we can achieve this kind of renewal.

May each one of us, by heeding the teaching of Jesus, be able to find once more the true value of his own existence and of the gifts God has given him for the service of all.

Holiness and Unity

> *'Holy Father,*
> *keep them in your name which you have given me*
> *so that they may be one like us'.*
> (Jn. 17,11.)

As is well known, these words are among the most sacred, most pregnant in meaning, most actual and modern of the whole Gospel message. Even a simple analysis reveals their infinite richness. 'Holy Father' are the first words. Jesus, naming the first divine Person as Father, reveals the significance of the divine message he came to bring.

God is not primarily truth or justice, nor is he primarily creator and benefactor; he is 'the Father' and he is 'holy'.

He is holy not with a holiness often understood by the Pharisees as a separation from all that is impure. He is holy with that holiness which Jesus came to gives us, with that spiritual reality which is within and springs from the

41

heart. And in God this spiritual holiness coincides with his very fatherhood. He is 'the Holy Father'.

The other word: 'Keep them in your name', tells us that he is not distant from the world, but that his holiness can and does intervene to sanctify the disciples of Jesus. Those who henceforth will be clothed with the new man. The new man who, in the image of God, is the holy man with an interior sanctity which will spill over into external works without exhausting itself in the trivia of the Pharisees.

And here Jesus adds: 'Keep them in your name which you have given me'.

We have already seen the value of the word 'name' in the mouth of Jesus. 'Name' signifies 'what you are'. This means that Jesus is saying 'Holy Father, keep them in your being', and he adds, 'which you have given to me'.

The mystery of the Trinity is enshrined in these words; indeed, in the Greek text, in just two words. The divine nature of the Father is completely poured into the Son and through the Son into the disciples, though in a different way. It is that same divine nature which sanctifies the faithful, makes them adopted children of God and leads them to holiness, keeping them, as the prayer of Jesus says, in this reality of the Trinity.

Then Jesus adds the nature of that holiness which penetrates the disciples from the Father and the Son. The holiness at which they must aim is 'unity', 'so that they may be one like us'.

What depth too in these words! The holiness that every Christian must attain, can be achieved by living in a manner analogous to that of the Father, the Son and the Holy Spirit. This is the holiness typical of Christianity. If for the Pharisees 'holiness' meant the fulfilment of many little complicated practices to stay pure; if, for a normally devout man, ignorant of Christianity, holiness may be the attainment of a deep personal union with God, for the Christian all that is not yet full holiness. His holiness will consist in immersing himself in the holiness of God, not on his own but together with others; it will mean reaching sanctity in unity with his neighbour. Only then will the Christian resemble Jesus, who lives in unity with the Father and the Holy Spirit. Only then will he live a specifically Christian holiness.

At a time when contact between members of the human race has become so close, when the social problem, that is the problem of relationship between man and man, dominates all others with its questions and its contrasts, now is the moment to rediscover what Christian holiness is. It consists in being united in the name of Jesus, in attaining in his name that fullness of divine life by which God appears not only in individuals, but in the living community which in this manner is immersed in God and in the Trinity.

People search for various solutions to today's problems, but the true solution will come to the world from the holiness God is arousing in his Church, that is from the unity that will come about among Christians. We fill ourselves with abstruse ideas and schemes, thinking thus to resolve the problems of the moment, yet it is in the apparently small spiritual things that the true solution is to be found.

It is in the 'yes' of Mary to the angel that the most overwhelming social revolution begins. It is the 'yes' of many Christians to the complete message of Jesus, to his testament, to his prayer for unity, that can signal the beginning of a deep and relevant renewal of the Church and of humanity.

In Dialogue
with the World

*'I have given them your word
and the world has hated them
because they are not of the world'.*
(Jn. 17,14.)

'I have given them your word and the world has
hated them because they are not of the world'.
The prayer that Jesus continues to address to
the Father at the Last Supper, is expressed with
the vision of the presence of truth in the world
and of the necessary opposition between the
word of God and sin.

In these days when we seek for continual
agreement between truth and the world around
us, these words of Jesus are bound to give us
pause. The revelation of Christ comes from God
and from on high, it comes into the world as a
most pure spring capable of raising people up
and making them children of truth. But at the
same time the word of God cannot but meet with
obstacles: 'the world has hated them'. And Saint

Paul echoed this: 'And all those who wish to live devout lives in Christ, will be persecuted'. (2 Tim. 3, 12.)

We must not delude ourselves. No compromise is conceivable between the mentality of Christ and of men. Here indeed, 'world' is to be understood in a negative sense. We Christians cannot live in a dream. A true accord between the children of light and the children of darkness will never be possible. The light, wherever it penetrates, will scatter the darkness and the darkness will try to extinguish the light. This truth throughout many centuries of Christianity has been clear and evident, manifested in its reality by the flight from the world, that attempt always made by Christians to be detached and separate so as to escape the contamination of evil.

And this truth has value today as well. Renunciation and detachment are indispensable conditions for preserving truth itself. No compromise is possible, no agreement between God and the prince of this world, between Christians and Mammon.

It is important to remember this fact at a time when dialogue with the world is so strongly emphasized. The dialogue with the world that is favoured by the Church and by the most sensitive souls, in no way nullifies Christian tradition. Today Christians, feeling themselves to be in possession of the truth, search in the world for people of good will who, without realizing it, are already children of the light. With them, it is possible to have dialogue and open one's heart to the common problems that torment mankind, because they too are often persecuted in the cause of justice, as they thirst after the God of truth who is Christ.

'Dialogue with world', though a necessity today and a duty for every Christian, must be given its true meaning. It will never be possible to have dialogue with sin, with lust, with avarice, with pride. In these there will be no possibility of any dialogue, since Christians will be hated and persecuted as Christ was.

The awareness the Church has acquired today, makes her able to distinguish between those who are of the world and those who are not of it. The children of this world, like the children of light, can be found everywhere – in the Church, among Christians, among non-Christians, and even among unbelievers. This is the discovery, if that is the right word, of the Second Vatican Council to have gone beyond external and formal divisions, so as to get to the heart of the matter. In this we follow the example of Jesus himself, who found good and bad among Jews and Pagans, among Samaritans and Pharisees. Jesus met with the children of light everywhere, just as he found among his own the son of perdition, Judas, who was of the world;

whereas Joseph of Arimathea, though a rich man, was not of the world. Neither was Nicodemus, though a member of the Sanhedrin. And neither was Gamaliel. Even though he provoked a distinction and an opposition between himself, his followers and the world, Jesus also entered into dialogue with the world in the sense understood by the Council. His mind and heart were open to everyone – and good and bad could be found anywhere. He says of the centurian: "Truly I tell you, nowhere in Israel have I found faith like this" (Mt. 8, 10.), and he works the miracle. Though not a Jew, the centurion was a child of the light and he too will have met with the hatred and opposition of the world, even of the religious world that considered itself close to God.

What thoughts, what examination of conscience this triggers off! We are Christians because we are baptized and believe, but are we true children of the light? Or are we attached to riches, to prestige, to glory? In this case we also will be children of darkness. We certainly cannot consider ourselves better than many non-Christians who work and suffer for greater truth and greater justice in the world. These are nearer to Christ than we are, if Mammon has made us its servants.

Living in the World

*'I am not asking you to remove
them from the world
but to protect them from the evil one'.*
(Jn. 17,15.)

As he continues to speak to the Father, Jesus uses
a word that can be translated in two ways: it
may mean evil or the evil one, the devil. The
Fathers used to translate this phrase: 'I do not ask
you to remove them from the world but to keep
them from evil'. Whereas modern scholars tend
to see in these words the personification of evil,
namely the devil.

This is not a serious difficulty, since in both
interpretations, one can include both diabolical
action and those works which lead directly or
indirectly to the devil.

Jesus does not pray that his disciples be
separated from human reality, but that they may
be preserved from its negative influences.

This verse also makes us ponder again the

49

whole Gospel message. The mystery of the incarnation demands of the disciples of Jesus not removal from humanity and from humanity's doings, even when these are evil or people are evil. We call to mind the other words of Jesus: the parable of the kingdom which is like a field where wheat and darnel grow, the image of the leaven in the lump, the parable of the fishes of the sea.

Only at the end of time will a clear distinction be made between the children of darkness and the children of light. On this earth there will always be a contact and a possibility of leavening the flour of humanity.

Jesus knows that on this earth no human being is now so completely perverse as to be closed to the voice of God. All are always redeemable and may be converted or improved. So he prays to his Father that his disciples may not yield to the allurements of wishing to separate now on earth what cannot be entirely separated: the good from the bad. Every person, however evil, will always have a thread of goodness in his soul, just as every person, however good, carries within himself that tendancy towards evil which is hereditary.

So it would be impossible to carry forward the kingdom of God by wishing to remove oneself completely from the world, even if this word be understood in its worst sense.

50

The message of Jesus is a message of salvation. Jesus is the doctor who has come more for the sick than the healthy. We should be that way too.

It is necessary to be personally separated from the influence of the evil one, but certainly we cannot therefore remove ourselves from human beings. Rather should we be the good yeast in their midst, being ourselves full of mercy, understanding and love, so as to find in all that pure vein of goodness, present in each one's heart. Through our love we need to reveal it to their eyes and to our own, so as to help people rediscover their true vocation and with it peace and happiness.

Let us look around. Have not we also expressed our judgement about many of those in our circle? Have we not often said, 'This one is open to the Gospel, the other is closed to it?'

If we have acted like this, we have already cut ourselves off. We have already desired to bring about that division which God has reserved to himself through his angels at the end of time.

Let us look at all with new eyes. All can come to discover the riches of the kingdom of God, even those whom we have already 'judged' in our hearts.

Let us remember always the words of Jesus: 'I have not come to judge the world, but to save the world'. (Jn. 12,47.)

Truth that Sanctifies

'Sanctify them in the truth;
your word is truth'.
(Jn. 17,17.)

At the Last Supper, Jesus has asked the Father to make his disciples 'one'. He has pondered the hatred the world will have for them and yet he has asked that they shall not be separated from the world. Now he asks that they be consecrated and made holy 'in the truth'.

If everything proclaimed and practised in the Old Testament is born in mind, the novelty is immediately apparent. Whereas people then were consecrated and sanctified in justice; now the disciples of Jesus are sanctified 'in the truth'. Old Testament justice was certainly not just legal and exterior. It too was rich with spiritual content, but it lent towards formalism, which by the time of Jesus, dominated the religious life of the Hebrews.

Jesus wishes his people to be consecrated 'in

the truth', made sacred 'in the truth'. Then he adds: 'your word is truth'.

If the Hebrews were introduced to justice from outside, through many exterior practices, in the New Testament everything will begin from within, from truth penetrating the soul of each of us.

We are not accustomed to the worship and exaltation of truth.

Truth is the acceptance of reality, that which is, by my mind and expressed in word. Truth is expressed in words, but first of all it is contemplation by the mind. And it is not easy to make our being adhere to truth. The evil tendencies left in us by original sin always lead us to pass over what really is, in favour of the distractions around us and the din of things. Or else we are distracted from the contemplation of truth by what is within us. We tend to adapt and scale down truth to our weakness, our sloth and our miseries.

When we look within ourselves, we often lack the courage to confront the truth which with a subtle voice makes itself heard in our soul. We try to forget it, suffocate it and drive it away. Listening to the truth speaking to us is a true asceticism. We need great self-control to be able to stop and listen, especially when the truth within torments and disconcerts us, demanding of us a radical change of life.

That is the moment when, if we are not attentive, we search immediately for an alibi, a justification for not listening to the truth. We see the people around us and we look in their behaviour for a pretext to console ourselves and justify our own. But we feel that the truth within is not content and is inviting us to a sincere examination of conscience, at least with ourselves, as to its demands and what we ought to do.

So, Jesus has begged the Father that the truth may sanctify us, that truth which pursues us wherever we are, which never abandons us and which we can never escape; that truth which, once accepted, reveals itself as the very Word of the Father, as the Word of God which, in his personal love for every individual, installs himself in our soul and illuminates and guides us in what each of us must do.

And once we have adhered to the truth, we feel ourselves inundated by that love which only the Father can give. 'If anyone loves me, he will keep my words and my Father will love him and we shall come to him and make our home in him'. (Jn.14,23.)

The True Root
of Holiness

> *'And for their sake I sanctify myself,*
> *so that they too*
> *may be consecrated in the truth'.*
> (Jn. 17,19.)

If we wish to bring its divine spiritual message to the world, we must discover the deep meaning of the Testament of Jesus with all its nuances, as exactly as possible. This is all the more necessary because modern words no longer mean what they did in ancient times. Instead of giving us the true meaning of the words of Jesus, they alter and change it because sometimes modern vocabularies no longer include words which exactly convey the ancient thought.

As is clear from an examination of this verse of chapter 17 of St. John, the translation says, 'For their sake I sanctify myself'. We tend to understand these words as an effort and a desire of Jesus to be continuousy holy in deed and word. This is, in fact, what we would do to sanctify ourselves – a continual effort, not always successful, to conform to a model.

This is not what Jesus meant to convey to us at the Last Supper, not only because, as Son of God, he was already holy in all that he said and did, but because in his day the word 'sanctify' meant 'to set aside for God'. This is precisely what is written in the book of Exodus: 'Sanctify all the first-born to me, the first issue of every womb among the sons of Israel. Whether man or beast, this is mine'. (Ex.13,2.)

It is in this sense that Jesus is speaking. He consecrates himself to God, thinking of the sacrifice of the cross about to take place. He offers himself as the first born of humanity, the Son of Man above all others, to become through suffering and death the victim mankind offers to the Father in expiation.

This will be the true root of the disciples' holiness. A holiness that before being a holiness in deed and thought, will be deep in their being, an ontological holiness like the very holiness of Jesus himself. So the last words of the verse become clear: 'so that they too may be sanctified in the truth'.

Here too the literal translation has altered the thought of Jesus.

In this phrase, Jesus wishes to tell us that his disciples will be made holy in truth, that is, really and effectively, and not so much by the truth, a concept he has already expressed in verse 17. Jesus has before his eyes the sacrifices of the Old Law, accepted by God even though they were exterior and valid only because they fore-shadowed the sacrifices of the unique victim, Christ, who will one day be offered. Such sacrifices made people holy but not 'in truth', as did the sacrifice of Jesus. They made people holy only externally and as a prefiguring of the future reality. Christ's sacrifice, however, renews man by actually turning him into the 'new man'.

Even if the example of Christ sacrificing himself to bring life to the world is unique and inimitable, yet his words also show us how we can be sanctified and sanctify others. It is done through the cross and through the consecration of ourselves as first fruits of mankind for the Father. We have to let ourselves be transformed by the passion of Christ into living members of his body who make the sap of divine grace flow. From the cross of Christ this will penetrate us and through the suffering accepted and offered it will expand, transformed into charity towards all who are near us.

Unity, the Crown of His Last Will and Testament

'I pray not only for these,
but also for those
who will believe in me through their word,
that they may all be one,
as you Father are in me and I in you,
may they be one in us,
so that the world may believe
that you have sent me'.
(Jn. 20,21.)

We may regard this saying of Jesus as the conclusion of his prayer to the Father. It seems to express the deepest and highest content of the Gospel message. In fact, it speaks to us of unity as the essential mark of Christianity, the deep life of the Church, and the apostolic witness of the presence of Christ in the world for the whole of mankind.

The Christian is united in God not through purification and intellectual contemplation, not through Neoplatonic ecstacy, but through faith.

In fact, Jesus prays for all those who will believe in him. The faith demanded of Christians is therefore possible and accessible to everybody. One does not have to be particularly intelligent, in control of one's senses and indifferent to all around. The school of Christ is very different from Eastern and Greek religious philosophies.

It is faith that saves and truth that penetrates the mind, coming from on high through the 'Word of God', and demanding in the listener an openness of heart, a loving readiness to learn and be guided, a humility in accepting the truth that sets him free and disposes him to act in a new way. For this reason the 'disciples' will be called 'faithful'. That is why Jesus prays that all may be 'perfectly one'. Never could merely intellectual teaching have obtained this result, since no human truth could ever so penetrate the depths of souls as to make them 'perfectly one'.

It becomes clearer and clearer that faith communicates to us a divine reality along with divine truth. In human affairs, concepts are separated and separable from reality. In divine things ideas and reality are identical. The word of God, passed on to us by the apostles, coincides with the reality of God given and communicated to us.

Now we also see the meaning of the other words of Jesus. This truth will make us 'one', 'perfectly one', 'as you Father are in me and I in you, may they be one in us'. It is the Trinity itself, Father, Son and Holy Spirit who communicate themselves through the word-reality. They take up their dwelling in us, raising us into their life of full unity and deepest distinction. Through this insertion of the divine-trinitarian life into us, we Christians will be 'perfectly one' and yet distinct from one another.

Often when we think of the mystery of the raising of the Christian into God, we are led to think of this elevation as exclusively personal, whereas the divine life is communicated to us in a trinitarian way, that is it is communicated to the individual and the group, simultaneously.

Human concepts and words do not manage to convey this mystery of the divine life on earth, since this is no more than a reflection of the trinitarian life.

So being united in the truth and in effective love is not a goal of perfection to be reached. It is a necessary pre-requisite. Hence the Church is not a future goal, but a visible reality, ever existing in past and present. The reality of being 'perfectly one' can and should be constantly perfected, but only as an evolution of something already existing, precisely because Christians are both 'perfectly one' and a 'multitude'.

Our spiritual life must free itself more and more from the limited Neoplatonic mentality which offers as exclusive goal the 'purified' individual who reaches the ecstacy of contact with the divine. Instead we must find our holiness of life in communion with Christ in humanity. This is the form of apostolic witness Jesus requires of us. Tiring ourselves out in human endeavour is not as important as the effort to allow God to be present in the world through and in the unity of brothers. Then he will be able to make the whole of mankind feel his presence, as he offers it the possibility of faith and salvation.

Faith, hope and charity in the New Testament.

Faith

'Lord, I believe'.
(Jn. 9,38.)

This word of Sacred Scripture comes from the marvellous passage of John's Gospel that describes the cure of the man born blind.

It tells us many things: God's way of acting in the world, his judgement of men, how a person can come to say, 'Lord, I believe', and who can reach this conclusion.

The occasion is a man born blind. The disciples ask Jesus what punishment from God makes him like this. Is it his fault, or his parents? Jesus, to set apostles free from their narrow human mentality, explains that this sad affliction is not the result of any personal sin but exists to display the work of God.

In this way, Jesus reveals how, beyond things that strike us and cause us pain, there is a divine logic that explains and transforms them. Divine wisdom makes us see earthly things with a new eye by removing the veil that human stupidity has drawn over the deepest reality.

John continues with an accurate description of the world's struggle between deceitful human wisdom, divine wisdom and the humble disciple who comes to believe.

This drama will unfold down the centuries. Here it is demonstrated in all its fearful harshness along the roads of Palestine, between Jesus who reveals himself in his divine sonship by means of the miracle of healing the man's blindness, the Pharisees whom human wisdom and culture blind completely, and a simple man of the people who lacks both education and culture, but whose heart is open to receive truth and so discover that it is God who is speaking to him.

It is a picture with all the elements needed to clarify the meaning of our faith and expose the cause of our unbelief.

It begins with Jesus revealing himself to the world in human form. God is with him, or rather he is God. His power which shines through all his actions, even the humblest and most simple, catches our attention and disturbs even the theologians of his day, more accustomed to reading the Bible and accommodating the revelation of God, turning it into a tool of their own pride, mediocrity and lust. They witness the miracle of Jesus, they see how effective it is in the world – with a little spittle and mud he restores a man's sight – but they do not wish to understand what is happening. They even go as far as to appeal to divine revelation, to Moses, to theological arguments in order to close their eyes absolutely to the vibrant reality immediately in front of them. They torment the blind man, upbraiding him for his malady, as if this made him a son of sin: 'You were steeped in sin at birth; how dare you lecture us?' (Jn. 9,34.)

The blind wisdom of men, full of themselves, tries to crush with the apparatus of learning the true intelligence and wisdom of anyone who sees truth and understands. It is then that Jesus reveals himself to the little son of Israel, cured of material blindness, persecuted and tormented by the Pharisees: 'He is the one who is speaking with you' (Jn. 9,37.), the Son of God.

Jesus, the miracle of healing brought about by his divine power, passes on to the total revelation of himself. He is the Son of God and the humble heart of the little son of Israel, whose mind is not suffocated by greed of heart, sees God in Jesus. He sees not only with the eyes of flesh restored to him, but above all, with his soul and kneeling before Christ in worship, utters that sacred word which makes him not only a disciple of the Master, but an adopted son of God: 'Lord, I believe'. His faith is understanding, born not of learning but of holiness of life. His faith springs from a tormented and patient humility. It is a clinging to God even in the struggle of the world that knows not God.

The scene ends with the terrible warning: 'If you were blind, you would not be guilty of sin; but now that you claim you can see, your guilt remains'. (Jn. 9,41.)

But these same words throw a ray of light and hope on a world that does not yet believe. Blindness, not yet having found faith, does not necessarily imply guilt.

It is self-sufficiency, pride and the corruption of the heart that turn blindness into crime, and in this case the judgement of Jesus is definitive.

We cannot read such pages of the Gospel without an examination being imposed on our conscience. Do we believe in the presence of Christ in the world? It is not simply a question of our mind accepting a well-ordered set of truths revealed by the Church. It is the discovery of Christ present and at work in the Church, in today's world, that we must make and perceive. Christ at work in his Church through the Church's ministers, Christ who awakens the Church through his presence at the Vatican Council, Christ who renews the Church through the charisms he is distributing.

It is Christ whom we must discover beyond

human events and the wretchedness of humanity. It is he who is at work in the world, within the Church and outside it, inspiring good even in a person who is still blind through no fault of his own. It is the problem of discerning wisdom in the midst of human things that imposes itself on each one of us with the same dramatic insistence as it did on the man born blind and on the Pharisees, whilst Jesus with saliva and earth plastered mud to restore sight.

If our sight were pure and limpid, we would succeed in fully understanding the events of our century with its travail, its revelations, its longing for brotherhood, justice and freedom.

Then we would understand the profound divine logic that links each day's trials, great or small, with a thread of gold.

But our heart is not always so limpid and pure. Self-interest, ambition and fear are mixed in with upright behaviour and good faith. Because the works we do are soaked in good and evil, our understanding has a fragmented, opaque and dull vision of the overwhelming presence of God in the Church and in the world. The veil of a human experience and wisdom keeps events, people and things hidden from us and, like the blind, we know only their outward shape and form which human touch can grasp.

It is then that the blind man falling to his knees with the words, 'Lord, I believe', seems the only possible reply to the action of Christ; even if many of us would like to add the other words, full of prayer and trust, of the father of the devil-possessed son which his trembling heart uttered for the removal of all impurity from his gaze: 'I believe, help my unbelief'. (Mk. 9,24.)

Inner Faith

'If you have faith and do not doubt....
even if you say to this mountain, "Go, throw yourself
into the sea," it will be done'.
(Mt. 21,21.)

Here the Gospel shows us Jesus working a miracle
which at first sight seems quite useless. After he
had spent the night at Bethany, he was once more
on his way to Jerusalem. He was hungry and saw a
fig tree beside the road. He went up to it to gather
fruit and not finding any, he said: 'May you never
bear fruit again'. 'Immediately the tree withered'.
(Mt. 21,19.) The disciples were amazed and asked,
'How did the fig tree wither so quickly?' (Mt.
21,20.) Then Jesus spoke those words whose
depth revealed the kind of faith demanded of
Christians, 'If you have faith and do not doubt . . .
even if you say to this mountain, "Go, throw
yourself into the sea," it will be done. If you
believe, you will receive whatever you ask for in
prayer'. (Mt. 21, 21–22.)

There is an obvious link between these events. Jesus works the miracle on the fig tree; the disciples are stupified because their faith in Christ is still superficial; they have agreed to follow him and join in his disputes with the theologians, the Pharisees, but their faith in the Son of Man goes no further than that.

This explains why Jesus looks for fruit on the tree and why he makes it wither. He wishes to awaken in the apostles a truer faith, a faith that springs from the very depth of their souls. His passion is near now and a superficial, exterior faith would be driven from their souls. The Lord wishes to prepare his followers for the approaching storm that is inescapable.

This is a new dimension in the understanding of Christ who could have prevented his disciples from scattering at the moment of the crucifixion. It is that faith which will allow Mary and John to remain at the foot of the cross without trembling and gather the last words of Jesus.

But the Gospel words widen our vision to a new dimension of the faith we must have. We usually think of this virtue simply as mental acceptance of the truth Christ offers us, and we are satisfied if we have overcome the doubts and trials that sometimes assail that acceptance. We are so tired of possessing the truth that we have no interest in penetrating it more deeply, simply because what we have is enough to satisfy us. Sometimes fear and laziness stop us from a deeper understanding of Jesus. A whole list of sayings has been invented to justify our faint-hearted and slothful Christianity: 'beware enthusiasm', 'hasten slowly', 'let sleeping dogs lie', 'don't overdo it', etc.

The moment the storm bursts upon Christendom, our faith, when nourished on these basically pagan maxims, is plucked from our minds and hearts along with those few truths we thought we possessed. Then superficiality, sloth and conformity appear in their true colours with all their meanness and repulsive narrow-mindedness.

That is why Jesus works the useless miracle of the withered fig tree, in order to shake off that crust of Christianity and reveal its heart to us. Our faith is not true and full and will not resist trials and temptations, unless it enters deeply into our souls to overflow into action.

The measure, to which Christian action must look as a goal to reach, was expressed by Jesus in the words: 'Even if you say to this mountain, "Go, throw yourself into the sea," it will be done'.

Faith enters us by degrees. Even when deep and true it can always be better expressed in concrete deeds, in proportion to the gradual growth of our belief in the revelation and divinity of Jesus.

There is no limit to this growth. It can come to a halt in the little doings of each day, or it can increase as the glance of our love discovers the world about us and its need of Christ.

It is then that the faith of the saints, not content to stand still in satisfied complacency, drives them on to work for God in an ever more intelligent and effective collaboration with him. So those giants of Christian life appear in the Church, starting great enterprises from nothing. St. Vincent de Paul, St. Joseph Cottolengo, Don Bosco, Frances Cabrini spring to mind.

Even secular history judges them to be geniuses; examining their lives, however, they often appear clearly as people like ourselves with their limits and defects. Yet faith in Christ has moulded and transformed them into great instruments in the plan of salvation and the story of mankind. Their deeply lived faith grew daily, hand in hand with the gift of themselves to God and to others, opening up the immense possibilities God had placed in their hands. St. Paul considers this charismatic faith as one of the gifts that the Gospel presents as available to everyone.

We recall the woman with the issue of blood: 'If I just touch his clothes, I will be healed'. (Mk.5,28.) And Jesus said: 'Daughter your faith has saved you. Go in peace and be freed from your suffering'. (Mk.5,34.) Or the episode of

Jairus: 'Don't be afraid, just believe'. (Mk.5,36.) The quotations could be multiplied. The whole Gospel is interwoven with miracles sparked off by the faith of poor people in Christ.

That is why we too can obtain from God all that is impossible to human power. How many insoluble problems each of us has carried in his soul for years! How many spiritual and bodily wounds have we dragged around with resigned acceptance without any light of hope reaching them! For us mediocre Christians who feel the weight of difficulties piling up, the Lord makes the fig tree wither. He who seems by that gesture to waste his divine power, is waiting for us to put it to good use. Christ, living throughout the centuries is always ready to use it for all Christians, for everything that is good and builds up the kingdom of God. Christ, the conqueror of physical and spiritual death, is simply waiting for our faith to enlarge and focus its trusting gaze on him. Then he will keep his infallible promise: 'If you believe, you will receive whatever you ask for in prayer'. (Mt.21,22.)

Hope

'May the God of hope fill you with all joy and peace'
(Rom. 15, 13.)

St. Paul often speaks of hope in his letters. At this point it seems useful to examine this sentence from Romans, since it makes clearer an essential aspect of Christian hope. Hope is a theological virtue, that is, its object is God. This verse brings out its peculiarity, its particular nuance of the love of God, in so far as hope is that love which returns and touches each one of us personally.

In faith, as well, the whole person is completely committed in its focusing upon God. And also with charity, it is man who tends with his loving being towards God as Father. But, to grasp fully the difference between faith, hope and charity, we have to come to see that in hope we turn to God for our own sake, in the sense that there exists a profound relationship between my happiness and my existence in God. This fact may prompt the question – in that case is not charity nullified by hope, since hope's element of selfishness excludes disinterested love, pure love? In reality, an examination of Paul's words and the essence of this virtue in depth, shows that this is not the case.

Hope expresses the relationship between God and his creatures. Hope tells me that God does not love me in an abstract way, but he loves me just as I am; he wants me to search for my happiness.

The difference between selfishness and hope is precisely this: in selfishness God is sought as the goal of our happiness, in hope happiness is sought as the desire of God. In egoism the balance of the God-creature relationship weighs in favour of the creature and so is opposed to God. In hope the balance is reversed and weighs in favour of God. He has certainly created us to serve him, but above all he wishes to give us the joy of delighting in eternal life.

And this is the deep reason for our hope in God.

In its primitive sense, hope indicates a desire, a complete tendency towards him who is everything for us, yet whom we do not yet possess because on earth the kingdom of God has not yet reached its full realization. Precisely because we are on trial, we face the continual risk of losing that absolute love which is our absolute joy.

We now see very clearly why we need hope, as

long as our life remains in its mortal and fallen state. Hope is precisely that virtue which comes to fill up what our human nature lacks to be truly and completely happy.

So Christian hope brings to fulfilment our desires for that absolute perfection, demanded both by our nature and by our supernature.

If, on the one hand, hope is the confirmation of our weakness and of our fleeting existence, on the other it is precisely this virtue that makes us fully human, giving back to us, in a real way veiled in mystery, that primeval integrity and satisfying that nostalgia for paradise which, ever since the fall of Adam, man will feel till the end of time. Then he will find himself once more with body and soul reunited in that absolute fullness of Christ who will return as conqueror of space and time, recapitulating both mankind and the cosmos in his own person.

Hope shares in all these divine and human riches through the infusion of joy. Hence St. Paul wrote: 'May the God of hope fill you with all joy and peace'.

Hope is necessary for survival in the tribulations of this life. It is hope that gives us the certainty of God's help. Even when trials and difficulties overwhelm us, through hope we know and feel they are already resolved, and that, if we so wish, they will never prevail in our earthly existence.

In moments of weakness, discouragement and

even sin, hope makes it possible to begin again, look towards God and get back on the road.

In his saddest moment – the saddest moment in the entire history of the universe and of all created being – hope could have brought Judas back into friendship with Jesus who still loved him; that relationship with God which could have filled the void created in him by his tremendous sin. But he did not find within himself that spark of salvation. By now Judas had evidently subordinated God and Jesus, on various occasions, to himself in his search for happiness. Happiness which he could only have found and regained by inserting himself into the divine plan. This is the heart of despair.

Despair cuts us off completely from God to the point where it becomes willed in our soul.

The opposite is to be found in St. Peter. He, in his way, had also betrayed his Master. By his act, he too is the personification of the sinner, but, unlike Judas, he feels himself to be a creature face to face with his Creator. Though sunk in the tremendous sorrow and remorse he must have felt, he had the courage to throw himself at the feet of God who, in that moment, was able to fill him with love again and give him back all his former joy and peace.

Down the centuries, the Church has denounced as mistaken all those doctrines which seem to offer a greater perfection, because they proposed pure love as the Christian goal. By pure love, these teachings meant a love devoid of hope. They went against the very essence of the love of God, because God loves us for himself and for our happiness. To desire such a pure love as to exclude ourselves completely is a total failure to grasp the mystery of the incarnation, the mystery of the very essence of God who is not a motionless ruler, but charity.

All of us need hope all the time. Even if we were to become perfect like the Church's greatest saints, never, on this earth, could we reach that fullness of the love of God and that possession of him that alone can truly satisfy us.

That is why hope remains even after death, in purgatory. And therefore there will be no hope in paradise. There faith and hope will be quite useless because God himself, making us know him face to face as he is, will finally fulfil our natural and supernatural desire for him. So Jesus never needed hope, though as man, we know from the Scriptures, Jesus suffered temptation in all things, yet without sin, and so he is our perfect model for all the virtues. The incarnate Word contained everything within himself, from the very first moment of his entry into the world.

All Christians should be characterised by joy and peace. Not a joy that does not know sorrow, but a joy that embraces and consumes it. That kind of joy which only Jesus can give.

Peaceful Hope

'And hope does not deceive us'
(Rom.5,5.)

St. Paul wishes to re-assure us that hope is not a vain, meaningless word. Hope is not the last straw at which we clutch in the face of despair.

Certainly, were we to think of this theological virtue in a human way, it would completely baffle us. It is not the refuge of those who, driven to the edge of life by internal or external difficulties, grasp at God and other people in an agonized search for help.

No, hope is not like that. 'It does not deceive', not simply because the Lord is absolute truth, and through an act of faith in his love and in his divine justice we are re-assured that he will always keep his promises. St. Paul wants to make us 'feel' and not merely believe, that it does not deceive. He wants our very being, our ego, to experience what hope is.

For Paul Christian life is not to remain a

theological formula outside the human person without touching its psychological life, the ego itself. That is why he describes the origins of that experience hope is to give us. He starts from concrete facts, from real circumstances in which each of us can find ourselves and in which we actually exist.

He says: 'And we rejoice in the hope of the glory of God'. (Rom.5,2.) But that is not enough. It would be little indeed, if we could only find a solution to today's problems in the future.

Paul's Christianity does not put off till tomorrow the solution of today's worries. In his view, it would be mean to look at life like that. So, he adds at once '. . . Not only so, but we also glory in our sufferings, because we know that suffering produces patience, and patience perseverence and perseverence hope. And hope does not deceive us, because God has poured out his love into our hearts by the Holy Spirit, whom he has given us. You see, at just the right time, when we were still powerless, Christ died for the ungodly'. (Rom.5,3-6.)

The logical chain of the argument is obvious to Paul, even if it comes to him in reverse order. Christ has died, even when we were powerless. Because of that, the Holy Spirit fills our hearts with his charity, so that when we are tested, 'feeling' his love which is already the kingdom of God in our hearts, hope springs up without deceiving us, because it comes from something we already possess. 'This test' to which we are subjected is the fruit of patience. In the long run, it must compel us to make a choice, and patience is caused by the sufferings of our daily living.

So it is logical for us to glory in our sufferings, because it is a boasting in the divine life that comes to us from the cross of Christ.

Only in St. Paul the description is the other way round because he presents this truth to us not as an argument but as an 'experience' that all Christians have and can exploit. That is why he starts from what we endure, our sufferings, and then proceeds to describe all the psychological stages of the Christian soul, in which he discovers patience and that hope which does not deceive, charity and the cross of Christ.

From his description we extract a theology of hope and charity, but how beautiful and vital was theology for Paul of Tarsus. It was an experimental truth, not an abstract idea to be explained to the faithful 'to make them believe' in something a long way off and detached from daily life.

To some extent, by extracting too much 'truth' from life, our statements no longer pass on 'truth'. This is because Christianity is not a mathematical system, but a truth which gives 'true life', which explains what it means to be human beings raised on this earth into the life of the Trinity. 'In him was life, and that life was the light of men'. (Jn.1,4.)

It is this hope we need, this hope we 'feel' to be certain, not deceiving us. Not because of theological studies, but because, in the confusion of our spiritual lives, made up of faith and charity, we see that God who reassures us is already present.

As long as we live, this assurance will never be absolute, not because of what God gives us and we experience from him, but because of our response to the gift of God. At the very moment fear of losing God appears and threatens to thrust us back into anguish, hope arises, gushing up from the soul to reassure us that the Lord is with us, inducing us to remain calm, trustfully abandoning ourselves to him.

The mysterious thing about hope is that it gives us both security and insecurity at the same time. This is precisely our 'trial' here below. It gives us peace whilst leaving us in fear that will no longer be 'terror' of God, but filial trust in him.

May the Lord always make us feel this 'hope' that does not deceive.

Charity

'God is Love'
(1 Jn. 4,16.)

All scholars agree that in the fourth chapter of his first letter, John reaches the summit of divine revelation.

St. Augustine comments: *'Bravis laus et magna laus, brevis in sermone et magna in intellectu'* – brief praise and great praise, brief in speech, great in understanding.

But what exactly does John mean by these words, the fruit of long years of meditation and prayer, once Jesus and Mary had gone to heaven?

I believe we have to confront their mystery with humble minds, if we hope to catch a glimpse of the treasure hidden in this jewel.

John had already said in his Gospel: 'God is spirit' (Jn. 4,24), and in this same letter: 'God is light'. (1 Jn. 1,5.)

If we were to consider these words, 'God is charity', with mere human understanding and imagine them to mean God is benevolence or goodness or sweetness, I believe we would begin to stray from John's thinking into a false piety and understanding of Christianity. 'God is charity' must not be understood in the sense we now usually give to that word. Its current usage has lost the primitive meaning it had in Christian language when the disciples of Jesus, and in particular Paul and John, coined this word to express the vitality and richness of Christianity.

They could not find an adequate word in the Greek of their day, so they took one, transformed and enriched it by giving it a very particular and precise meaning. We could say that they invented the word *agape*, even if something similar was used before to speak of both human and religious love. But for Paul and John, this word no longer had its usual meaning. For them love did not mean something sweet or courtly. It was a concept of life. Christian *agape–love* took the very meaning of man, exalted it, raised it and made it dynamically alive and directed towards others, not merely in external deeds, in concrete works, as a simple communication of one's own faith. For John and Paul, charity was everything for man and not just a giving of himself in spiritual and material acts.

Paul had written in his first letter to Corinth: 'If I speak in the tongues of men and of angels, but have not love, I am only a resounding gong or a clanging cymbal'. (1 Cor.13,1.)

Therefore Christian charity is something grafted into human nature, uplifting and making man a 'new creature'. Yet charity must not be thought of as something opposed to human nature, almost as if grace were an alteration of what man is by nature. No. When divine charity enters man, it makes a harmonious synthesis with his natural tendencies and aspirations. In fact, both nature and grace have issued from the hands of the same God. Hence the *agape–charity* of Paul and John seizes and invests the whole man. That is why Paul said: 'If I have not charity, I am nothing'. (1 Cor.13,2.)

He could not say this, if charity were just an external attitude, a moral way of living, or a quality which springs from the supernatural man. No. In the Christian view, charity takes hold of the whole man; if he does not love, it is as though he did not exist.

This deep reason makes charity one with the very notion of being and human existence. But if this idea of charity, as the New Testament presents it, touches the very being of the creature, it is simply because man shares in a certain way in the *agape–being* which is God. So in the minds of Paul and John, we pass from man to God and from God to man. In fact, a little earlier John says: 'Dear friends, let us love one another, for love comes from God. Everyone who loves has been born of God and knows God. Whoever does not love does not know God, because God is love'. (1 Jn.4,7-8.)

'God is charity' does not merely indicate that God possesses love, as he possesses justice, strength, power. John could have written, 'God has charity', or, 'In God there is charity', and these form a perfect unity in him who is utmost simplicity. But John did not say this. He wished to make quite clear to us what is the intimate nature of God's being. His being is love.

This is precisely the mystery for us, since when we think of our being, we always see it as something separate and distinct from love, and when we think of love, we always see it supported by something that already is. But to think that being is love, to think of God as love, this is indeed mysterious.

Hence our profound need to deepen yet more our understanding of Christianity, which is not merely a knowledge of ideas but an experience of life. On this point John has not the slightest doubt: 'Whoever does not love does not know God'.

We are so accustomed to stressing, indeed over-stressing the value of the human soul which is really very simple, when we are talking of knowledge, that John's words may seem to be just metaphors, allegories or a literary style adapted to the first century after Christ, when the Gnostic crisis imposed a particular language. No. We must also bear in mind that John wrote those words by divine inspiration. We must remember that they were dictated by the Holy Spirit, and reflect that they have been handed down unchanged by the Church through the centuries, precisely because they are intended to teach the twentieth century something as well.

We too need to put reason and love in their proper places, in the way John offers them to us. We know if we love. If John wrote those words in that form because of the Gnostic crisis, as some maintain, then we must admit that we in this century are also affected and infected by our own gnosis: by reason which desires to smother the spirit, by the rationalization which desires to restrict and force revelation into rigid, dead, formulas.

We must not alter the genuine sense of the significance of the words of Paul and John. 'God is charity'. We need to meditate and.live them to understand them. Then we shall perceive how Christian revelation has a profound and vital ideology all its own, an ideology that cannot be so simply identified with Platonic or Aristotelian philosophy. The philosophy of Jesus can surpass and absorb both the one and the other. It is our reasoning that must reach up to the level of God.

It is not for us to bring the revelation of God down to man's level of thinking.

Hence the need for humility. Hence our need to approach these words of John with trembling souls and purified minds and hearts. Purified not just of sensual attachments, but of intellectual attachments too, so as to let ourselves be inundated by that divine light which is both love and being, life and wisdom.

Charity within Man

'With your whole heart'
(Mt.22,37.)

Matthew's Gospel reports this saying of Jesus, explicitly connecting it with one of the Pharisees' numerous attempts to find an opportunity or pretext to accuse Jesus, or at least to embarrass him in front of his crowd of listeners.

To this end, the Pharisees, seeing how he had reduced the Saducees to silence, gathered together. It was a council meeting, dictated by hatred and malice, disguised as unctious devotion and holiness, as zeal for the kingdom of God. They chose one of their number, a doctor of the law, a professional theologian to checkmate the master of truth.

With the meticulous scrupulosity of spiritual accountants the Synagogue had enumerated 613 commandments. These were divided into 248 positive and 365 negative precepts. These interminable lists were in their turn divided into

95

light commandments which could be expiated by penance, and serious commandments punishable by the death penalty. Naturally, among these light and serious faults, there were lighter and grave infringements. So it was logical that, wishing to oppose Jesus, the doctors of the Law should put questions prompted by their spiritual level, their intellectual plane and pre-occupation with narrow, ridiculous problems. So the question is put to the master: 'Which is the greatest commandment in the Law?' Jesus replied: 'Love the Lord your God with your whole heart and with your whole soul and your whole mind. This is the first and greatest commandment. And the second is like it. Love your neighbour as yourself. The whole Law and the prophets are reduced to these two commandments'. (Mt.22,37-40.)

At a stroke, the Pharisees' 613 precepts vanish into two commandments which in reality are only one.

We know the impressions made on the Pharisees who had concocted a minute plan of attack to trip Jesus into theological error.

As it turned out, his reply was on another plane, from another world. Everything became simple. Religion itself which appeared to be an unbearable source of scruples and misunderstandings, became accessible to everyone. It was understandable and attainable by all however illiterate, even without the list of precepts. Religious life was a relationship between man and God, and among men with God.

But every word of Jesus which sums up the law and the prophets for us, claims our loving understanding in depth, so, if possible, we desire to grasp the true meaning of the word 'heart'.

What did this word mean in Biblical language, in New Testament vocabulary and in the teaching of Jesus? Besides referring to the human organ in the chest, in the common acceptance of Hebrew thought, *the heart* indicated the unity of the primary psychic life of man, that unity which constitutes each one of us as man before being body and soul. In the Bible, the heart is the centre of the human being, the source of his behaviour. It is not only the centre of affection, but also of thought and will.[1] It is into the heart that God infuses wisdom,[2] and the heart is the place of decisions.[3]

The devout person is not divided in his heart,[4] whereas the wicked person is split within himself.[5]

---

1 'I commune with my heart at night; I meditate and search my spirit'. (Psalm 77,6.)
2 'The whole world sought audience with Solomon to hear the wisdom God had put in his heart'. (1 Kings 10,24.)
3 'From what you have, take an offering for the Lord. Everyone who is urged by his heart bring an offering for the Lord'. (Exodus 35,5.)
4 'I will give them singleness of heart and action, so that they will always fear me, for their own good and the good of their children after them'. (Jeremiah 32,39.)
5 'Their inquity bursts from their eyes, the evil conceits of their hearts knows no limits'. (Psalms 73,7.)

It is the heart that expresses true authentic religion, before any external rite, even before any external action. In New Testament thought, the heart is the place where 'as yet there is no distinction between body and soul, action and intention, the inner and outer man . . . it is the very source of his personality, the mystery of God'.[6] Therefore Jesus tells us that we must love with the whole heart *(kardía)* with the whole soul *(psychē)*, with the whole mind *(diánoia)*.

Man, whose faculties are secondary, is primarily and essentially a unity and it is with this intrinsic and unified gift of himself that he turns to God. That is why St. Paul prays, in his letter to the Ephesians (3,16-19): 'that out of his glorious riches he may strengthen you with power through his spirit in your inner being, so that Christ may dwell in your *hearts* through faith. And I pray that you, being rooted and established in love, may have power, together with all the saints, to grasp how wide and long and high and deep is the love of Christ, and to know this love that surpasses knowledge'.

It is precisely into the heart that our faith comes to insert itself, faith communicated by grace, to the heart understood as the unity of man, through which the intelligence will then understand a little, and the will develop its love.

---

6 Cf. K. Rahner, *Enciclopedie dela Foi,I.* Coeur.

But, even before we can love and know, Christ has to dwell in our hearts. It is he who, pouring his love into us, transforms us completely, raising us up and enlightening us. Love understood in this way will become the source of knowledge. It is this heart that Jesus demands of us in order to love God and he wishes that everything *(olé)* be given to the Lord. Not a fibre of our psycho-somatic being, that is our body and soul, should remain excluded from this total choice of God, from this complete turning to him which is our duty. He is above and beyond every other precept. He sums up for us every other command of the law of the Old and New Testaments. He unifies us and simplifies for us the Christian life in all its apparent multiple commitments, but which in reality are reduced only to taking hold of us in the fullness of our existence and directing us in total unity to God.

Therefore, scruples, religious traumas, and petty details should be banished from our personal lives and religious practice. God asks something much simpler of us, even if this is a great deal more. But just because it is simpler, the very young and children, men of the people, old and illiterate folk can understand it easily. Whereas this truth can remain hidden from the learned, the clever, and the professionals of human and theological science.

Loving God with one's Life

'Love the Lord your God with your whole soul'
(Mt.22,37.)

As we have seen, these words of Jesus were a clear and simple reply to one of the Pharisees who had attempted to put the Master to the test. 'Which is the greatest commandment?' And Jesus had replied: 'You shall love the Lord your God with your whole heart, your whole soul, your whole mind'.

In our efforts to understand these words in depth, we have seen what 'heart' *(kardía)* meant in Jewish and New Testament thought. A similar analysis is indispensable for this word 'soul' *(psychē)* as well.

What meaning did it have for Jesus? This question is all the more important because in the Western world the word 'soul' has by now acquired a very definite and particular significance. For us the soul is the spiritual part of our person, that part which has the powers of intellect and will. It is precisely this that will survive death and has been defined as the form of the body, that is, the informing principle of our human nature. This is why we distinguish between body and soul with great ease. By now these words are everyday language with a precise meaning. Some might deny the survival of the soul, as unfortunately the materialists do, but even they distinguish between soul and body, although for them the soul is not spiritual in our sense.

But let us try to grasp what the Hebrews understood, since Jesus had quoted the command to love God from a Hebrew source, the book of Deuteronomy (6,5). There we discover that besides loving him with the whole heart, we are to love God with the whole *nefes*, which we have since translated into modern languages with word soul. Further research soon shows us that in Hebrew thought, *nefes* was something very different from our soul.

Nefes came from the verb 'to blow', 'to breathe'. So like the word *heart*, it had a material meaning, namely throat, though in common usage it meant a great deal more. Hence *nefes* indicated the breath of life and the vital force. So in the Old Testament we often find *nefes* used to indicate a living being – man, animals. It is the normal centre of the feelings of love and hate, but also of desire and concupiscence.

In addition, some would see in this word

vegetative and sensitive life as opposed to the spiritual life, but this is not easy to sustain, since in the Hebrew thought there was no true distinction between soul and body in the Greek and Western sense. That is why we rarely, if ever, find a survival of the *nefes* outside the body after death. It is not that the Hebrews denied human survival, which is clearly affirmed (Proverbs 2,18;21,16; Isaiah 14,9), though not in the sense we now understand it. For that we have to wait for the Book of Wisdom, written in Greek, when there existed adequate tools of language to express what we mean by the immortality of the soul.

Nefes does also mean 'soul' in our sense, but always as united to the body. Therefore, when the New Testament speaks of the 'soul', using the Greek word *psychē*, it often has a Hebrew significance. It may indicate physical life (Mt.2,20) or life which implies all earthly and heavenly goods (Mt.16,26.). That is why Jesus can say that he who wishes to save his soul *(psychē)* will lose it, whereas anyone who loses his soul for Christ will find it (Mk.8,35); simply because the soul *(psychē)* meaning life has acquired particular shades to designate the origin of feelings and acts of will. Not that 'will' is to be understood in our technical sense, but in a much fuller sense, as the attitude of man with all his feelings, with the whole of his desire for good. It is in this sense that Jesus said that God must be loved with the whole soul *(psychē)*.

Jesus did not tell us just to make acts of love for God, nor simply to show charity in deed towards our neighbour. Jesus desired the whole of our being and existence to be turned to God and to our neighbour, in a fullness and with our whole personality, which only living can make us fully understand. Then our love will not be just affection or sentiment, though it will include them; not just a thing of decision and will with a great effort of our ego, though it will consist of that too. It is our very existence in its pursuit of the good that Jesus demands of us whole and entire.

Sometimes, in order to emphasize the purity and nobility of religion, we are led to distinguish our faculties too neatly, splitting off the spiritual from the sensitive will and even thinking of affection as a negative thing to be repressed and destroyed. Jesus does not ask this of us. Jesus simply wants us to give everything to God. We stand in need of purification in so far as original sin urges us to centre our affections and feelings on creatures, instead of bringing them to God and turning them over completely to him.

Christian life is not meant to be a destruction or diminution of man. The good and the holy which God has created and given to us must remain complete. It can only remain pure and holy if it is given first of all to God and if other people are loved in God and with God.

Loving God with Intelligence

'Love the Lord your God with your whole mind'
(Mt.22,37.)

We have witnessed Jesus quoting the Old Law from Deuteronomy, in reply to the Pharisee's question. This inculcated the duty of love of God with the whole heart, soul and strength.

But we have seen that whereas 'heart' meant above all the unity of man, whether in his affections or in his thinking, 'soul' in that passage meant man considered as will, both spiritual and sensitive, the two being clearly bound and integrated.

In Matthew's text we do not find the words: 'with your whole strength'. These come from Mark and Luke (Mk.12,30; Lk.10,27). But evidently the three evangelists realized the difficulty of translating into Greek the entire depth of meaning contained in the words spoken by Jesus. So they added our need to love God with the whole mind *(diánoia)*.

They knew that the Greek world would not have fully understood the Lord's command, if they had only given a literal translation of the Hebrew. In Hebrew 'heart' and 'soul' also involved reasoning, the typical exercise of the mind, which was not so in Greek. For the Greeks, *diánoia*, namely the faculty of thinking, had the technical sense of reasoning.

This meaning has remained in Western languages, in which of itself 'mind' indicates neither feelings nor will.

I have tried to analyse very briefly the differences between the original Hebrew and the text of the Gospel, precisely so as to understand, as far as possible, how we are to love our Lord.

A submission of our intelligence is required of us. Often man is led to think in a godless way (Eph. 4,18) as he ponders his life, the world, the people around him and reason itself, from his own perspective with his very partial and very limited intelligence. If man were to desire to keep for himself this mind, this reasoning of his, if he refused to submit it to his Creator who is Mind itself, he would risk ending up understanding nothing.

To love with the mind is to give our mind to God.

To love with the mind is to recognize the limit of our thinking and reasoning.

By doing so, man is not performing an

irrational act, does not become less human, does not enter an anti-human obscurantism, rather does his reason enter new dimensions, dimensions like those of God.

The apostles who had to translate and pass on the message of Jesus to that Greek world which had developed reason in a sublimely deep way, felt the need to recall precisely in Greek that the *diánoia*, the mind, had to be completely surrendered to God.

In some ways, the century in which the apostles lived, was rather like these last centuries in which we Christians have found ourselves. In Europe too, at a certain moment, people thought that reason, ratiocination, human intelligence could give us all the answers, could explain and illuminate life and the very mystery of God.

Man grabbed at his own reason, to make himself independent even of God. What has been his experience? We all know it, suddenly we have all felt the sufferings and catastrophes and wars and crises of man who had not wished to surrender his own reason, who had not wished to love God with all his *diánoia*.

We have often witnessed the collapse of this Western civilisation. We have witnessed, and still do, the killing of many people and of entire races just on the strength 'a reason', of human thinking which looks for an excuse, which searches for a justification of not living in God.

107

We have witnessed and we are witnessing reason wreaking destruction, man who wishes to save his greatness by intelligence ending up brutalized and destroying himself in despair.

These are the fruits of reason which desires to keep its independence of God, refusing to bend, not wishing to give itself to God.

Sometimes, this mentality has infiltrated Christians too. In certain expressions of our lives, reason is a myth we wish to preserve because we think that by hanging on to it, we can, in a human sense, save something.

In reality, our mind can only reason if it allows itself to be completed by the light of God. Its human capacity then becomes a supernatural capacity. That divine light given to us, completes and raises even purely human reasoning which without its submission to God is so easily led to reason falsely.

The Word was God.

As we Christians seldom recall, it is only by abandoning ourselves completely to God that we can find an equilibrium even in thought.

But I would like to emphasize that the Lord asks us *to love* God with our whole reasoning process.

We are so accustomed to separating thinking from loving in modern languages that the apostles even appear to be saying something strange; with the reason one thinks, not loves, we are tempted to say. And yet the apostles had used the word *diánoia* precisely to indicate reasoning, uniting it expressly with the word love.

Even reason must love.

This is the deep secret hidden in these words of the Gospel. Words that only a life in God and for God can glimpse and grasp a little. Without a life in and for God, reason cannot understand that it must love and only understands that it must think, and by limiting itself to thought, it reasons falsely.

Love of God

*'Because the effect
of the love of God is to make us keep
his commandments'*
(1 Jn.5.3.)

We have seen how in Matthew's Gospel Jesus faces us with the commandment to love God in all its fullness and totality, as proclaimed in the Old Testament; and we know how he linked this with love of other people. In fact, he concluded: 'In these two commandments are contained the whole law and the prophets'. (Mt.22,40.) We have also noted the linguistic nuances used by the evangelists to give us the full content of the command to love God, as it was expressed in Hebrew. Now these words of John lead us to the link between the love of God and love of neighbour.

The Holy Spirit, in Sacred Scripture, not only wished to show us the two fundamental aspects of our religious life, but also to give us a simple, practical, concrete rule which we can all understand and apply in order to have a real love of God and a true love of our neighbour.

Since God is invisible and beyond all experience of the senses, the love of God could become a meaningless word.

So we are told: a man cannot love God whom he cannot see, unless he loves his neighbour whom he sees. (1 Jn.4,20.)

But if the love of God is in danger of becoming an illusion, and risks expressing itself in external practices of devotion, empty of true meaning, unless it is proved by an effective love for other people, so too love for other people has its risks and ambiguities.

Love for other people can become a theoretic philanthropy, selfish possessiveness, or romantic affection empty of any true content.

If we had to analyse the word 'love' in current use, we should find that it has the most varied meanings, with thousands of nuances and indications of different attitudes of mind. In fact, this word is so rich in content, so full of the human and the divine, that in contact with the language of men it fragments into all manner of applications and deviations. Because of this, the Holy Spirit wished to put us on our guard, by giving us a sure means of knowing when our love for other people is true and a share in the loving fatherhood of God.

All this is handed to us in the above sentence of

John. In its full context it reads: 'Anyone who believes that Jesus is the Messiah is born of God, and anyone who loves the Father loves the Son whom he begets. By this shall we know that we are the children of God: when we love God and keep his commandments. Because the effect of the love of God is to make us keep his commandments, and his commandments are not difficult, since everyone who is born of God overcomes the world'. (1 Jn.5,1-4.)

This passage evidently includes various directions, all linked together. We are given a definition of the Christian: he who believes that Christ is the Messiah, that is, that Christ is the Son of God. By this faith we are born of God, that is, we are made sharers in the divine sonship.

It is heart-warming to note that birth from God is not a passing event, as with human birth, when once children are grown up, they go their own way. No. When we are born of God, we go on being born. We never cease to receive being and life from the Father.

The Greek word used here is the passive past participle, which shows exactly how the one who receives divine life continues to remain dependent for his existence on the God who is loving him. So it is logical that the one who is generated cannot but love the others generated by the same God. John says: 'Whoever loves the one who generates, also loves the one who is generated'. This word contains the revelation of the metaphysical motive for love among human beings. We are co-generated together. Therefore we have the same nature. So love, the divine *agape*,[1] can be truly born amongst us, for inasmuch as we are in 'being', we are so because we participate in the divine *agape*, as generated children.

Mutual love is not limited to its moral, spiritual and ascetic aspects. Love between human persons has a deep philosophical meaning. It gives the only true light on the reason for our co-existence. At this point, John, to warn us of other possible interpretations of human love says: 'Because the effect of the love of God is to make us keep his commandments'.

If the love of God for us leads us as a logical consequence to love for other people, so love for others, if it is true love, ascends immediately towards God, and the confirmation of this is our keeping the commandments. When we imagine that we must draw back from God's commandments in order to love our neighbour, that means that our love is not true love of neighbour. It is already mixed up with ourselves, even if this self-interest appears disguised as benevolence, broad-mindedness, sentiment or philanthropy. These are all terms that hide a lack of true love for

---

1 Cf. the chapter entitled 'Charity', p89

one's neighbour. Sometimes they contain exhibitionism disguised as philanthropy, or a tacit agreement to leave our neighbour in his defects so as to avoid being forced to remove our own, such as laxness of attitude, or egoism, such as that sentimentality which we give to others in order to get something for ourselves.

The sure test of our true love which is also truly human, is its constant harmony with the commands of God. This involves a morally pure life, detachment from riches, and a search not for success of the applause of man, but for the gift of oneself in humility and obscurity. Then John says: 'God's commandments are not difficult'. 'When we love', says Augustine, 'either we don't get tired or the tiredness is loved'.[2]

For anyone who loves, the Lord's commands are, in fact, light and gentle, since they are in harmony with the direction of our existence. Whereas they become heavy, difficult and painful, only when our will, even unconsciously, is not directed to God but to something else. The Lord's commands, of their nature which is entirely in harmony with the development and perfecting of the human being, are not oppressive, even if grace needs to conquer concupiscence, the legacy of original sin. We shall discover in their fulfilment a harmonious development of

2 Cf. 'The good of widowhood', 26 PL 40.448

ourselves, our personality. We shall feel 'fulfilled' and not 'frustrated'. Frustration belongs to those who fix their lives on the world instead of on God.

This is why John can tell us: 'Everyone who is born of God overcomes the world'. Living in the acceptance of his love and receiving life in the exchange of love, strengthens us to overcome all difficulties within, and, without, mis-understandings, mockery and the persecutions natural to Christians. A profound joy will then invade our souls, almost an assurance that the difficulties are a sign that we are in the love of God, as Jesus declared in his sermon on the mount: 'Blessed are those who suffer persecution for justice's sake'. (Mt.5,10.)

Persecution and difficulties from the world carry a special joy, the joy of feeling ourselves to be children of God and as such keeping Jesus company on the cross.

Love of Neighbour

'Love your neighbour as yourself'
(Mk.12,31.)

What did Jesus mean when he spoke of 'neighbour'? No idle question this, since by 'neighbour' we mean someone who lives near us. From that comes the meaning of 'neighbour' as someone who is spiritually near, a person whom I treat as my friend. In this sense we often say: 'one must do good to one's neighbour', 'we must love our neighbour'. But what exactly did Jesus understand by this word? His hearers asked him and put the same question: 'Who is my neighbour?' (Lk.10,29.)

In the Old Testament this word refers especially to a relative, either by race or because he has been assimilated by the Hebrew people. It implied a bond of blood or juridical relationship, consanguinity acquired by acceptance into the Hebrew community. That is why Jesus, by telling the story of the Good Samaritan that

117

we all know, wished to make clear his understanding of the word 'neighbour'.

In Christian revelation, neighbours are not just those who are spiritually close, nor simply relations through family or nationality. Jesus takes as his model a Samaritan, that is someone from afar, belonging to a different religion, another people, another race, in order to show how for Christians, all who belong to the human race, even if they do not share our religious moral or political ideals are, and must become, our 'neighbours'.

So we must think it all out again, if we are to put new life into this word of Jesus. We do not live with Samaritans, we have nothing to do with Pharisees or Romans or Greeks. Our neighbours are our mates in the factory, our colleagues in the office, our superiors at work or school. Our 'neighbours' are those who do not yet understand the meaning and value of Christianity. Even more, 'neighbours' are those who believe it their duty to spread scientific atheism through-out the world. Even those who corrupt society by the systematic and commercial propagation of immorality are 'neighbours'.

Therefore we have to love them too. Each of us has his difficult and his easy neighbours. It may be that our next door neighbours are spiritually the furthest away; it could even be that it is just these to whom we should feel closest, whereas we wish to treat them as foreigners. Our permanent temptation is to restrict the words of Jesus to certain types of people. This temptation is linked to human nature's desire to escape suffering and reject the cross. In that case, we unconsciously and involuntarily read the Gospel without understanding it, restricting the value and weight of Biblical phrases. Neither must we be at peace, once we have discovered the meaning of the word 'neighbour'. No. Every day we need to ponder it again and begin again to fill this discovery with life and vitality. Every day we have near us people to love, serve, help. But in what way are we to love our neighbour?

This phrase from the Old Testament, taken up by Jesus again and explained in a new way looks simple and easy enough: 'as yourself'. 'As yourself' certainly means not doing to others what we would not wish them to do to us. But to avoid doing evil to one's neighbour is simply the negative aspect. Jesus does not just say this; he tells us to *love* our neighbour *as ourselves*. And loving certainly means doing the good we would like done to ourselves. But even this is only one aspect of the content of Jesus' sentence, namely that of material charity and service of others – giving one's money, one's energy or one's time, so that others may benefit therefrom. All this is definitely contained in his command, but he wants even more. He wants us to give others our spiritual possessions, that we love them as ourselves, helping them to understanding the value of the Christian life, leading them to discover that Christ is the Son of God and that we are all brothers in the kingdom of Heaven.

So loving our neighbour as ourselves necessarily implies a living and effective Christian witness, and not just the corporal works of mercy. So we have to learn from Jesus and put ourselves in his school. Jesus is surely the Master who has shown us with his life how one acts to bring Christianity to others. Loving others spiritually as oneself does not simply mean preaching or catechising. These spiritual works of mercy are certainly important and necessary. They show us one aspect of how to love our neighbour, but if we ponder the motive of the Word taking flesh, that is of the life of Jesus, we realize that he came to die on the cross, and so to give us his life.

So loving truly *as oneself*, means taking our Lord as our model and being ready to give our life for our neighbour. *Giving one's life* is the extreme possibility of the greatest love of neighbour, but implies a total attitude of our existence launched towards others. It implies not clinging to ourselves, not worrying any more about ourselves, being always directed towards the good of others, and having as our only anchor and guide God who gives us the power and possibility to love others.

Then we shall realize that loving *as oneself*, involving our whole being, makes us live again the life of the Father, the Son and the Holy Spirit, makes us repeat a little the total gift of the Father to the Son and of the Son to the Father. It makes us discover that beneath these words, written in Leviticus hundreds and hundreds of years before the coming of Jesus, a life is foreshadowed, a life which will be revealed by Jesus as the intimate life of the Trinity. We must love others as ourselves because God loves *as himself*. Herein lies the mystery of the Trinity.

These words are then revealed in all their mysterious depth. They announce beforehand all that Jesus will say on the eve of his passion. 'Holy Father keep them in your name. . . so that they may be perfectly one like us'. (Jn. 17,11.)

Universal Love

'Love your enemies and pray
for those who persecute you'.
(Mt. 5,44.)

One aspect of love for our neighbour which requires deeper meditation, both because it is rather difficult to put into practice and because it throws a new light on the revelation of charity, is the command of Jesus: 'Love your enemies and pray for those who persecute you'.

At first sight, the enemies of Christians seem to be an easy problem to solve. Often they are those who persecute missionaries or other members of the Church in countries where religious liberty is crushed.

To some extent they are certainly our enemies too, but on deeper reflection, we realize that they are not *our* enemies, but the enemies of the missionaries or of Christians deprived of their liberty. They are only our enemies through the spiritual union we feel with their victims. In reality they are not our enemies.

If we look around us, *ours* are not represented by a category, they are not groups of people of a particular ideology or political complexion. Generally speaking, our enemies are much more concrete and a good deal less important. Precisely because they are *our* enemies, they are much closer to us, sometimes living in our own homes, office or school. They are of the same nationality, our fellow citizens, and often share our religious, political and moral ideas.

So a little thought shows us clearly who our enemies are. We all know there are people at school or at work who prevent our colleagues and superiors knowing and appreciating us. We can immediately identify the person who gets in the way of our career, or who circulates rumours at our expense through subtly poisonous jokes.

Sometimes they are people who hold different religious or political views, but these are rather marginal enemies.

Often our enemies are people we have offended by our way of acting or our wicked way of life, and now they are 'resented' for all they have received from us. Or else they are simply envious folk worried about saving their position in the little society in which we live together.

So our enemies are those who 'have it in for us'. No need for imaginary or hypothetical enemies, nor for romantic feelings of solidarity with the victims of suffering world wide, thus avoiding having to face up to the real difficulties of every day.

Our enemies once identified, we realize what our Lord is saying: 'Love your enemies and pray for those who persecute you, so that you may be sons of your Father in heaven'. We do not read: 'let your enemies get lost', 'don't get upset by your enemies'. The Gospel command is much more serious and demanding; it obliges us to do something positive towards our opponents.

How often we hear even Christians say, 'I'll do him no harm, even if he has got it in for me'. That is not a truly Christian statement, but one that smacks of stoicism. Christianity goes further and puts love where there is hatred; it builds something where there is a lack. We must not content ourselves with not acting negatively towards our neighbours. We must not rest at peace until they have become our friends, that is until we have succeeded by our love in filling the emptiness of their lack. Then we shall often realize that besides their failures, our own are part of the problem.

We need to pray, too, for anyone who persecutes us. Here we are speaking of religious persecution. Sometime, or perhaps often, we Christians are led to defend our ego, our interests, our pride behind the mask of religious principles.

Jesus puts us on guard against this temptation.

Not even spiritual motives can justify our not loving our enemies. Even more should we then work and pray when we are truly persecuted for religious reasons.

But it is not always true that those who oppose us, do so for our religious feelings. It often happens that they are attacking our laziness, our slothfulness, our presumption rather than our religion. They are persecuting a false image of religion to be found in our lives. Without our realizing it, they are asking us to live up to the faith we have embraced, the Creed we say in words that we wish to live.

Frequently, our difficulties do not arise from the world's hatred of Christianity, but from the repugnance men feel for our deformation of religion. But if others wished to persecute our faith, even when we are being consistent before God and men and sincerely doing what we profess to believe, even in that case religion itself induces us to love even more, in order to bring God to them too.

Then we shall be true children of the Father in heaven who sent his only Son to redeem the world at the very moment when men were in rebellion against him. We shall become children of that Father who considers no one as lost and makes the rain fall and the sun rise upon the evil and good, so that all may have time to repent, feel his love and discover his fatherhood.

And this is what God is waiting for from his children: that we may always be in an attitude of love with our enemies and his, so as to help the Father in heaven to re-unite all mankind as one divine and human family.

Mutual Love

'This is my command,
that you love one another'.
(Jn.15,12.)

On the eve of his passion, Jesus summed up all his teachings in the simplest words ever used by any thinker: 'Love one another'. They contain all his theological, philosophical, spiritual and moral truth.

They are words anyone can understand from the least educated to the most scientific and cultured. They enter into every dialect and language, surpassing all Eastern or Western, Arab or Semitic cultures. Everybody grasps this saying, since love is the mystery of the origin of life among men.

In fact, it is from the love of two people, husband and wife, that children receive life and the society of the family is born. It is the mutual love of parents and children that permits natural human development, both physical and psychological. And it is these words, even though not often put into practice, that permit a certain co-existence in civil life. This is why they are immediately understood by everybody. Scarcely are they uttered than all people realize their truth embracing the mystery of human happiness.

Very often, while pondering the Lord's command, we remain only on the level of the affections and psychology or simply on the moral and spiritual level.

Whereas these words enshrine the deep secret of the mystery of being. If all people of every race and condition have immediately understood these words; if they have, in fact, a very real value in the everyday lives of families and peoples, it is because, beyond all this, they have a deeper value still, a value that touches the very nature of being. They express the philosophy, the metaphysics of the Trinity. In fact, being and mutual love are the reason why God is God. It is unthinkable that another God exists other than he, and God is One and Three. This means that he is God because he is in the mutual love of the Three Persons. It is through this same love that we receive from God, moment by moment, our very existence as creatures and as human beings. That is why each one of us can love God in return, why each one of us can live these words of Jesus with him.

But this love that God pours out again,

giving us being, does not limit itself to the free personality of each individual. At the same time God loves us, giving us being 'together with other persons'. He gives us existence in such a way that among ourselves we can live something of that mutual love that circulates between Father, Son and Holy Spirit. God gives this gift to mankind as a whole, of which each person is at once a part and a free individual on his own. Even if this gift only finds its complete fulfilment in the life of grace shared by us, its basis already exists in human nature and natural human co-existence; even naturally God shares a little of his being with us.

Now we can understand how love between human beings is the true, secret mainspring of the human generation of children, of the birth of families and peoples, and of the co-existence of all mankind.

The Gospel is not just a book of religious devotion, but one that contains divine wisdom made human. These two sources of wisdom are neither divided nor opposed. The one longs for the other, and the other fulfils this longing, perfecting and raising it up. It is this interlacing of human and divine wisdom that is shown us in the Bible, and particularly in the New Testament, it is enshrined by Jesus in this short, very profound sentence, which seems as simple as the life of God is simple, even in its greatest and most absolute mystery: 'Love one another'.